The Ultimate Philosophy

by *Jon Will, ESQ., CPA, MBA*

PublishAmerica
Baltimore

© 2002 by Jon Will.
All rights reserved. No part of this book may be reproduced in any form without written permission from the publishers, except by a reviewer who may quote brief passages in a review to be printed in a newspaper or magazine.

First printing

ISBN: 1-59129-818-0
PUBLISHED BY PUBLISHAMERICA BOOK PUBLISHERS
www.publishamerica.com
Baltimore

Printed in the United States of America

DEDICATION

Every human dreams of a better life.
This trilogy is dedicated to Humanity's Dream.

THE ULTIMATE PHILOSOPHY - BOOK I

A Map To Utopia

Introduction

Humanity is evolving from praying to God, to playing God.

Table of Contents

Chapter I	The Facts of Life
Chapter II	Religion Is A Myth
Chapter III	Utopia
Chapter IV	Fundamentals for Utopia
Chapter V	Everlasting Life and Good vs. Evil
Chapter VI	Basics of Life
Chapter VII	The Individual and Society
Chapter VIII	Knowledge
Chapter IX	Faith
Chapter X	Summation

Chapter I
The Facts of Life
"Existence is Truth"

Everything we know of is the third dimension, and its properties. Everything is composed of atoms, and atoms are composed of smaller particles. All particles are three-dimensional because they have the dimension of height, the dimension of width, and the dimension of depth. Air is composed of particles in a low state of density, water is composed of particles in a more dense state, and physical objects are composed of particles in a high state of density. This universal sea of particles in different states of density, is the third dimension.

The third dimension exists because from all of the infinite possibilities only it could exist. Fourth or higher dimensions cannot exist because a space cannot be overfilled, in the same way that two separate three-dimensional objects cannot occupy the same space at the same time. A zero dimension, or nothingness, cannot exist, because there must be something for there to be an existence, and subsequently, there must be a dimension. The first and second dimension lack existence on one or two levels and therefore exhibit the properties of nothingness, and, as such, they cannot exist. Consequently, everything, which is infinity, must be three-dimensional. Therefore, if one travels away from earth, in any direction, they will always be able to continue traveling further. There is no end to either the largeness or future of the third dimension since only it can, and therefore only it will, always exist. There is no beginning since only the third dimension could exist and therefore always did exist. This is the Infinity Theory of creation.

The Big Bang Theory is currently the generally accepted scientific theory of creation, which requires the universe to be finite since there was a beginning, and would require that time be a dimension. But time has not been proven to be a dimension. There are all kinds of theories about other dimensions, and speculation that there may be as many as eleven dimensions, but the simple fact is that only the three dimensions of height, width, and depth have been scientifically proven to exist. While some things, such as time, appear to be other than three-dimensional, they are in fact nothing more than elements of the third dimension. Time is not a dimension, but simply a property of the continuing change, in the third dimension, caused by the interaction of objects in the third dimension which constantly moves forward from the state the objects are in to their new state of existence. This forward motion, which is simply a phenomenon of the third dimension, is measured by man through designations such as minutes, hours, days, and years.

The fact that the surrounding section of universe which we can see is expanding, is used as evidence of the Big Bang Theory of creation. But there are other possible explanations for this expansion. For example, we see the creation of life on earth everyday, such as when a sperm and egg combine they grow. If our solar system was a small part of this type of transformation on a larger scale (such as an atom in an embryo) then we would see an expanding universe. But this would be a transformation of matter in our section of the universe and not creation of everything there is.

It is plain common sense that a magician does not really make a rabbit appear from thin air, and it takes an even more unrealistic leap of faith to believe that the 200 billion stars in our galaxy, and over 100 billion galaxies in our seeable section of the universe, popped out of thin air as alleged by the Big Bang Theory. Also, to believe the universe is finite would mean there is an edge to the universe which presupposes there is some barrier at the edge, or that one will fall off into nothingness in the same way humans use to believe the earth was flat. Every time we develop new methods to observe deeper into space, we find there is more space.

Math of the Big Bang Theory, 0 = everything, does not equate.

But math of the Infinity Theory, everything = everything, does equate.

The only rational creation explanation is that there is an infinite sea of three-dimensional particles, with no beginning or end, both as to time and size. Subsequently, Humanity's creator is nothing more than what could and what always did exist, the third dimension. As part of the third dimension's infinity, humans became one of the infinite combinations therein.

Chapter II
Religion Is A Myth
"Heeding Idols Is Wasted Effort"

What is the one true religion? Whichever religion is selected, all the other religions believe that religion is wrong. Therefore, the only universal agreement among all religions, is that they do not believe in each other. Subsequently, all religions agree with atheists, except when it comes to their own religion. Since there are over 3,000 different faith groups around the world, each religious person is 99.97% atheist toward Humanity's religions.

Since the truth of Humanity's creation is simply that humans are one of the infinite combinations in the infinity of the third dimension, it must also be true that all religions, which all allege creation of man by a superior being, are based on a falsehood. Religion is a crutch which can be easy for an individual to lean on when life becomes tough, but as a falsehood will not truly support Humanity as evidenced by the multitude of problems, pains, and sufferings which continue to plague earth, even though religion has been in existence for a long, long, time. Religion did serve a useful purpose, in times when man was less knowledgeable about the universe, by filling the void of ignorance with a positive message which also taught societal values and peaceful coexistence. However, these religious seeds have grown in the darkness of ignorance to create divisions between people with various religious beliefs, which divisions create conflicts based on religious differences and fuel the fires of hatred and discrimination. This dark side must be dispelled by the light of truth which exposes the false prophets of religion. The only gospel which should be preached is the true gospel of Humanity, which is that all Humans exist in the common house of the third dimension, where no gods exist.

Chapter III
Utopia
*"Anything is No Longer A Puzzle,
Once All of Its Pieces Are Put Together"*

Once the truth is known, it becomes self-evident that Humanity is simply on a journey through the third dimension. When one is on a journey they should know their destination. Since every human dreams of a better life, Humanities common destination should be Utopia, which is what religion refers to as heaven, and which is the best existence obtainable. Since the truth is that one will not be handed the Utopia of heaven on a silver platter simply by worshiping a false god, then it must be concluded that Utopia will only come through Humanities own efforts. Humanity can and must make its own path in the third dimension. Humanity should strive to make its own heaven, a heaven on earth, a Utopia. Only a unified belief and effort by humans will bring Utopia, a heaven on earth, to Humanity. Humanity's true salvation is through the unified pursuit of Utopia. Utopia can happen if you ask not what Humanity can do for you, but what you can do for Humanity.

The first step on the stairway to Utopia is to define what Utopia is, and thereby set forth what goal Humanity should strive to reach. Utopia is generally defined as a place of ideal perfection in all aspects of existence. Once Humanity knows Utopia is the house it wants to live in, Humanity can begin to build that house. Since Utopia is the blueprint for Humanity's house, the next step is to determine what materials are needed to assemble that house. There are five basic elements to Utopia. These elements are:

1. Everlasting life;
2. All good and no evil;
3. Infinite provision of all tangible and intangible needs and wants for existence, without any required effort to obtain those provisions;
4. A perfect balance between the individual and society;
5. Complete knowledge.

Chapter IV
Fundamentals for Utopia
"Only the Enlightened Will Comprehend the Light"

Once the elements for the house of Utopia are identified, the next step is to establish basic working principles to use as tools to create the needed materials for Humanity's home. However, before the basic working principles can be established, one must have an understanding of some basic human fundamentals.

No individual could exist without some interaction with other humans, and Humanity will only survive if there is interaction of humans. Therefore, it is fundamental that a society in some form will always be necessary.

While no two humans are exactly alike, all humans are equal in the fact that they are all part of the same species, and all humans come from a common beginning through their evolution into existence from the infinity of the third dimension. Subsequently, red or yellow, black or white, tall or small, young or old, shy or bold, all humans are equal in the realm of their creator, the third dimension. Therefore, it is fundamental that all humans are equal in the eyes of society.

Every human consists of both a tangible physical existence and an intangible mental existence. The tangible and intangible parts co-exist as one being. A human's mental state is capable of positive or good thoughts, and negative or evil thoughts. Additionally, the mental state can cause the physical state to act upon any type of thought. Subsequently, humans can be evil to varying degrees. Since societies consist of humans, societies can be evil to varying degrees. Therefore, it is fundamental that both individuals and societies must contend with the continuing battle of good versus evil.

In summation, it is fundamental that humans live together, as equals, in a positive and good way. While some people would say that if this occurred, it would be Utopia, they would be wrong, because this simply consists of building the foundation on which to build Humanity's house of Utopia. Any house is only as strong as its foundation. If Humanity does not have this strong fundamental base, any attempt at building a Utopia will crumble.

Now that the foundation has been laid, the basic working principles can be addressed. Basic working principles must be practical and suited for the current condition of Humanity, and therefore flexible for change as the condition of Humanity advances toward the Utopian condition. With this understanding in mind, four basic sets of working principles are set forth in the following four chapters.

Chapter V
Everlasting Life and Good vs. Evil
"A Brief Time of Love is Worth More Than an Eternity of Hate"

Since good and evil are so interwoven with life, the basic working principles for these two elements of Utopia must be applied to both elements as one.

While humans may be the superior intellectual beings on the planet earth, that does not make human life superior to all life in the big picture. Human life could not exist on earth without the existence of other life forms on earth. Humanity must currently exist as part of a food chain. While other life forms may be required to nourish and sustain humans, humans should respect those life forms. Destruction of another life form without valid purpose is wrong, and cruelty to any life form is always wrong. Of course, once Utopia is achieved, synthetic foods or other technologies will change this equation.

On an individual level, people must overcome the negative emotional shortcomings of Humanity. Hatred, jealously, malice and other negative thoughts must be controlled and should never be allowed to control one's actions. The results of non-control are verbal and/or physical crimes against other persons or physical crimes to others' property. Infliction of physical harm on another human is always wrong except when done to stop physical evil. Emotional harm caused by malicious acts such as verbal abuse, theft, or destruction of others' property is always wrong. One who engages in any of these wrongful acts not only fails to respect the value of others' life, but also fails to respect the value of their own life. In addition to controlling the negative side of human nature, the individual should focus on positives such as love, generosity, and achievement. If all individuals stopped committing crimes Humanity would be well on its way to Utopia. However, some individuals are inherently evil, and this is where society must fill the void. Those humans who engage in evil acts, and who cannot reform their behavior, must be taken out of society permanently, by one method or another. At this point in time, society has limited resources, which leads to the conclusion that instead of wasting fertilizer on these weeds of society, the weeds should be pulled, and resources should be directed toward assisting good people in need, so that the flowers in the garden of Utopia may flourish.

Every individual affects Humanity as a whole in that one's actions have a ripple affect through society in the same way a splash ripples through a pond when a stone is thrown into the pond. While some people make a bigger splash than others, such as Hitler's big negative splash, and Einstein's big positive splash, every splash is important, because each splash affects Humanity, with the negative splashes pushing Humanity toward a living hell and the positive splashes pushing Humanity toward Utopia. Progress toward Utopia can be accelerated if everyone avoids making negative splashes, and instead makes as big a positive splash as they can. While humans currently have a physical limitation of mortality, one does obtain a form of eternal life in that their splash is an everlasting effect on Humanity. Once Utopia is reached, there will be physical immortality through cell regeneration, memory transfer to a robotic humanoid, or some other method beyond our current knowledge.

Chapter VI
Basics of Life
"An Infant Crawls Before It Walks and Walks Before it Runs"

All religions should stop wasting their energies on theological differences, which are all false and therefore irrelevant, and instead work as one organization dedicated to the true mission of advancing Humanity toward Utopia. The tremendous resources of all the religious organizations combined, refocused on this mission, could accomplish miracles. This united charitable organization could start with the promotion of food, clothing, medical care and shelter for all, which would be a giant step toward Utopia. Religious organizations could join with governments and other private organizations in utilizing the religious halls of prayer as warehouses for a united effort in collecting and dispersing food and clothing to the needy. Religious buildings not operating as warehouses could be converted to temporary residence halls for the homeless while building supplies are collected in the converted warehouses for volunteers and the needy to utilize in converting vacant lots and abandoned buildings into suitable housing for the homeless. Training centers, job placement services, referrals to available medical care, and access to all types of helpful information could be consolidated under this charitable umbrella to assist people in regaining self sufficiency when needed, or maintain survival when self sufficiency can not be reobtained. If there was a consolidated effort by all who are now providing such services in a piecemeal and fragmented way, the basic goal of food, clothing, medical care and shelter (a guaranteed minimum living level) could be obtained by Humanity as a whole. This minimum living level must also encompass humans mental state. At a minimum level, those who are mentally dysfunctional to the point where they cannot provide for their physical needs, must get help from society that will rectify the dysfunction so as these individuals may obtain the ability to at least provide for their physical needs for survival. Of course, more than the mental minimum should be done, such as providing human interaction for elderly people living alone. These are basic working principles that will change to increase the scope of the guaranteed minimum living level as Humanity moves closer toward Utopia.

It should be noted that even if religious organizations do not want to give up their false beliefs, they still could combine some of their efforts under a united charitable organization for the advancement of Humanity. One does not have to give up their religious beliefs in order to believe in Utopia. In fact, that is one of the reasons why Utopia is so beautiful, because in Utopia everyone is free to believe what they want to believe.

Chapter VII
The Individual and Society
*"The Whole Cannot Exist Without the Parts
and The Parts Cannot Exist Without the Whole"*

There must be a government of some sort for humans to peacefully coexist. Only government can provide mechanisms for peaceful dispute resolution for parties who cannot resolve their disputes. Only government can provide necessary infrastructures such as roads. Without governments to enact laws to regulate the various interactions of humans, there would be total chaos.

The structure of government must change with the times. As the earth becomes technologically smaller, (where once it took weeks to cross the Atlantic Ocean in a ship with a message, a phone call can now be placed in a matter of seconds) the nations of the world must have more cooperative interaction. Thus, as city and town governments are to state governments, and state governments are to national governments, so must national governments be to a world government.

Each national government must allow its citizens certain basic fundamental freedoms. The general rule on fundamental freedoms is that anything should be allowed so long as others are not adversely affected. The standard for determining what is an adverse affect should be determined by each society as a whole. Each society should make their determinations through a purely democratic or representative democratic form. Dictatorships and one party systems of communism do not allow for society to make their own determinations. Additionally, capitalism is currently the most proficient system at creating productivity, and capitalism can only truly survive in a democracy. Therefore, the form of government should be self-government through democracy.

It is a basic principle that government promote the advancement of Humanity toward Utopia. Governments are responsible for enacting laws that encourage good and discourage evil. Governments have the power to promote the advancement of knowledge. Governments, through their actions, affect the marketplace, and therefore have the ability to enhance Humanities standard of living. Governments should consolidate their charitable programs, (such as welfare, unemployment insurance, food stamps, aid to dependent families, etc.) and coordinate the efforts of these programs with the united charitable organization discussed in Chapter Six, in order to establish a guaranteed minimum living level based on the current resources of Humanity.

Currently, individuals must sacrifice some of their freedom in order to live in society, such as for example not being able to play loud music in an apartment building. Additionally, even if one lives in a free society, their freedom is limited by the need to earn a living, which subjects them to spending time in a dictatorship environment if they work for an employer, or the slavery of being tied to operating their own business. Eventually, robots, computers, and machines will be able to perform all work that needs to be done, and by themselves create unlimited production capabilities, which will free humans from the binding chains of earning a living and therefore allow humans the true freedom to pursue happiness and fulfillment. This unlimited production capability and technological advancement will also allow for the solution to the problem of limitations from living in a society, such as providing sound proof housing so that one can blast music without adversely affecting others. Once Utopia is achieved, it would be possible for each individual to live in an environment that suits whatever needs and desires that individual has. Everyone would have their own heaven.

Chapter VIII
Knowledge
"The Holy Grail"

Knowledge is the cornerstone for achieving Utopia. Knowledge permeates the other basic working principles and all of the Utopian elements. Knowledge in the hands of good people can stop evil in any of its forms. Knowledge can lead to surplus food supplies and cure illnesses. Knowledge can stop pollution and create faster and safer forms of transportation. Knowledge can find the means for human immortality. Knowledge can lead to unlimited production capability and therefore a top-of-the-line standard of living for all humans. All of Humanities problems can be solved by knowledge.

Humanity must continually support and encourage the pursuit of knowledge which can provide Humanity the technological ability to live a physically and emotionally safe and fulfilling life. The most daunting frontier Humanity faces is the frontier of ignorance which must continually be conquered through research and invention in all fields of science. The economic incentive of the reward of profits through patent protection of successful inventions is a currently viable system of encouragement. Yet only society as a whole through government is able to undertake and fund technologies where business would not or could not proceed, such as space exploration. Greater cooperation, coordination and effort must be undertaken by governments, educational institutions and the business community, to advance the pursuit of knowledge. Everyone should also strive individually to increase their knowledge and encourage their children to pursue the path of knowledge so that both the individual and society as a whole reap the rewards that knowledge can bestow. The pursuit of knowledge is one basic working principle that should never change, but once obtained, may change other basic working principles, and even Utopian elements.

Chapter IX
Faith
*"Blind Faith is Dangerous,
Informed Faith Is Miraculous"*

Some people will say Utopia is an impossible dream. If you set your sights on only grabbing a leaf off of a high tree limb, instead of grabbing for a star, because you believe the leaf is more attainable, then you will only get the leaf, which will wither and die, while the star still shines from afar. History is full of happenings that naysayers said would never happen, but that dreamers made happen. Without dreams, new frontiers never become reality. All people dream of a better life. Admit to that dream and join in the wish upon the star of Utopia. One who has this faith will reap the rewards of a better life.

Have you ever played the wishing game, the game where you are asked what you would wish for if you had three wishes? The ultimate answer, with just one wish, is to wish for a Utopia for everyone. Let us make this wish come true.

Humanity has the potential to accomplish anything that does not violate the fundamental parameters of the universe. Fundamental parameters are scientifically demonstrated limits, such as the fact that two separate three-dimensional objects may not occupy the same space at the same time. Utopia is a human invention, and as such is not a fundamental parameter of the universe. Therefore, Utopia can be achieved.

Chapter X
Summation
"Only A Conscious Effort Will Achieve the Desired Result"

All I am saying, is give Utopia a chance. Humanity can have a better existence. First believe, then work toward the belief. Humanity as a whole, has the whole world in its hands. It is time for Humanity to embrace the promise of its future as it enters the 21st century. May the force of the third dimension be with you, and may all live long and prosper.

Proceed ye then as a positive splash.

THE ULTIMATE PHILOSOPHY - BOOK II

The Light of Knowledge

Introduction

The first book, The Ultimate Philosophy - Book I, established the simple premise that since it is up to Humanity to make its own way, and everyone dreams of a better life, we should work toward Utopia, which is the best life attainable.

That book then set forth a map which showed a path for reaching Utopia.

This second book sets forth some ideas to facilitate walking the path toward Utopia.

Table of Contents

Chapter I   Consensus
Chapter II   Best Use
Chapter III   Wisdom
Chapter IV   Discovery
Chapter V   Fix the System
Chapter VI   Wise Spending
Chapter VII   Simplicity
Chapter VIII   Roots
Chapter IX   Try
Chapter X   Summation

Chapter I
Consensus
"Common Goal"

"Utopia" is simply a word used to define what can generally be described as the consummate dream of the best level of Human existence. Every person has thought, at least once in their life, that it would be nice if there were no disease, no crime, no poverty, and/or for some other improvement in the Human condition. Since everyone has dreamed of a better world, it is fair to say that Humanity has a common dream. However, instead of recognizing our commonality, we have created artificial differences among ourselves through concepts such as nationality and religion. While no two humans are exactly the same, we are all of one race, the human race, and we all share the experience of life in an essentially identical carbon-based life form structure. We all work for continuing survival while in this structure, and hope for a happy, safe, and good life for ourselves and loved ones. Therefore, everyone has a common desire for the best life attainable. Since Utopia offers the best life, we should jointly try to achieve Utopia.

Additionally, it should be noted that without a goal, happenstance determines a traveler's destination. Instead of leaving its fate up to chance, Humanity should select its own destination for its journey through time. If one has to choose a goal, it might as well be the best. Since Utopia is the best life attainable, it is the best goal for Humanity.

The first step in reaching a common goal is to identify and agree upon the same. Humanity already has a consensus for a better world, and simply should recognize this fact. The next step, after a consensus is reached, is to take action toward the same. Therefore, Humanity should focus its efforts on reaching its dream of Utopia.

Chapter II
Best Use
"Resource Realignment"

Knowledge should be the focus of Humanity's efforts, because knowledge is the key to Utopia. With the right knowledge, we can cure all illness. With the right knowledge, we can feed the hungry. With the right knowledge, we can stop pollution. With robots, machines, computers, and new technologies beyond our current knowledge such as molecular rearranging mechanisms, we can have unlimited production capabilities. With the right knowledge, we can solve any problem, and achieve any desired result. In sum, Humanity can achieve Utopia by simply accumulating sufficient knowledge.

History has shown that any time Humanity wants to learn how to do something, such as land a man on the moon, the answers can be found if money and resources are devoted to the cause. One desired technology is cheap and clean energy. Sunlight provides more energy than Humanity could ever use, we just need to find how to harness the same. Plus, solar energy is environmentally clean. A massive research effort could find the answers to this cheap and clean source of energy within a relatively short time. If we had started such an effort during the gas shortage 25 years ago, we would probably have this technology now. Once the savings and benefits of abundant clean solar energy are achieved, those freed resources can be rolled back into other beneficial research, and any freed resources from the results of that new research can be rolled back into other beneficial research, etc. until we have Utopia.

Knowledge is like a snowball rolled from the top of a snow-covered mountain. It starts small, but exponentially increases. In the last 30 years more information was processed than in the previous 5,000 years. If Humanity recognized this reality, and devoted more resources toward acquisition, dissemination, and use of knowledge, we could accelerate the pace at which we reach a better world.

It should be noted that knowledge and technology are not synonymous. Technology is simply a tool that can be used when the benefit to society exceeds the benefit of other methods. If natural methods provide the best results, then clearly they should be used over manmade methods. Knowledge is cognition of truth, insight of justice, awareness of the best way, and wisdom in behavior.

The rest of this book proposes some ideas for resource realignment toward the goal of Utopia. Resource realignment simply involves finding current ways that effort and material are being used wastefully, and then diverting these efforts and materials toward the most productive use. Since the ultimate goal is Utopia, and knowledge is the key to the goal, then as many resources as possible should be diverted toward knowledge. The following resource realignment ideas are not exclusive, so please feel free to develop other ideas, and disseminate that knowledge for the benefit of all mankind.

Chapter III
Wisdom
"Use from Awareness"

The three basic ways of interacting with knowledge, are:

1. acquisition of new knowledge from research, through experience, or from other avenues of discovery;
2. dissemination from accessing stored information, through teaching, or from other methods of communication;
3. use through actions based on awareness of knowledge.

The remainder of this chapter will discuss dissemination and use of knowledge. The next chapter will discuss acquisition of knowledge.

Humanity has achieved proficient methods for dissemination of information, and thereby means for easy access to use current knowledge. Computers offer an efficient and economical way to store information, and the Internet provides a method for fast and easy access to information. However, the full potential of the Internet is not being utilized. The solution could be a master website for each area of man's accumulated knowledge, a virtual library of all accumulated knowledge. For example, in the field of medicine, the American Medical Association, in cooperation with universities that teach in the field of medicine, could create and maintain a website which contains all knowledge about medicine, so that anyone could access the information. Government should initiate a consortium effort in conjunction with organizations, institutions, and/or industry to create a master website for each area of knowledge, or encourage the creation of such master websites through financial incentives and/or financial support. Such a system has minuscule costs in comparison to the benefits that could be derived therefrom. The full power of current knowledge could be unleashed by such a universal system providing fast and easy access to Humanity's accumulated knowledge.

Dissemination of knowledge includes education. Everyone benefits from education, both the individual taught and society. Yet universities continually increase the costs to obtain higher education, even though means exist for providing education in a more efficient, accessible, and economic manner. Most degree programs simply consist of courses comprised of the reading of a textbook, discussion of the same in a classroom, and the taking of tests to show knowledge of the subject. It would be a savings of both time and expense for one to attend college over the Internet, via a virtual school system where one learns from computer programs developed by the best educators. Such a system allows each person to learn at their own pace, from the comfort and safety of their home. The time and expense of commuting to and from school, or residing at school, would be eliminated. The expense of school land and buildings could be eliminated. In fact, all expenses could be eliminated, except for the cost of the computer programs, the cost of online experts to provide student assistance as needed, and the cost of administrative staff to oversee the system. Reducing economic and other barriers to education, and the better life it generally offers, should be the goal of every public school system. An education revolution is easily available through current technologies that provide the means for people to learn more, at less expense, and with greater ease. Any teachers displaced because of implementation of an Internet school system should be offered research jobs, where they could continue using their expertise by seeking new and better knowledge for the advancement of Humanity. The expense of these new research jobs can easily be funded from the savings resulting from a virtual school system.

Technology has opened the door for cheap and easy access to knowledge, which includes education. The public has a right to the accumulated knowledge base of mankind, and that right includes access to the same without having to hurdle prohibitive economic barriers. The Internet is technologically accessible anywhere in the world, and transcends political, national, and other boundaries. Those who cannot afford their own home computer, can find access to the same at public libraries, and should have their own system if needed through methods such as education loans, charitable programs, recycling of discarded machines, etc. Any and all means to provide access to knowledge so that people can increase their wisdom, and thereby increase their ability to have positive instead of negative impacts with their actions, should be pursued. Knowledge is power, power to the people.

Chapter IV
Discovery
"Knowledge Exploration"

The ability to have Utopia simply requires acquiring the right new knowledge. Subsequently, a comprehensive global effort to discover new information in all fields of knowledge is highly desirable. Other than discovery by luck, most discovery of new knowledge results from "research and development" (R&D). Therefore, Humanity's knowledge can be increased by simply increasing funding for R&D. While knowledge infrastructure, such as easy access to information and an increased education level, will facilitate research for new information, money is needed for scientists, physicists, engineers, etc., and the equipment they need, in order to find new knowledge. Less than 2% of current global productivity is being devoted to R&D. Clearly Humanity could and should be investing more in its future.

Top priority should be devoted toward discovering methods that may allow Humanity to leapfrog knowledge acquisition capabilities. Some such methods are discovering how people can use more than the 10% average of brainpower, or how to make computers that think. If all people could think at genius level, the capabilities of invention and creation would exponentially increase. Computers with thinking ability could develop new knowledge from large volumes of data. Thinking computers would provide the ability to build robots that can perform labor tasks, which would free more resources for R&D.

Individuals, industry, governments, universities, and nonprofit organizations, are the different type of entities engaged in funding R&D. All of these entities can find ways to increase the amount of resources devoted to R&D. Individuals could make and/or increase their donations to organizations funding research to find beneficial knowledge, such as medical cures. Individuals can undertake their own invention efforts, or increase such efforts already undertaken. Individuals can become expert in a field of knowledge and find a research job in that field, or start an organization for the same. Industry is by far the largest spender on R&D. Therefore, financial incentive to encourage both industry and individuals to pursue R&D must be continued through venture capital systems, patent systems, and other viable systems that encourage these privately funded R&D efforts. Industry could utilize research consortiums to increase the effectiveness of their R&D investments. Governments could increase their funding of R&D by eliminating wasteful government spending and reinvesting those savings in R&D, without any additional sacrifice to the public, and with a huge potential benefit from the same. Universities could consolidate, and/or move toward a virtual teaching system, and refocus any savings therefrom on finding new knowledge. Nonprofit organizations engaged in R&D could consolidate and/or find other means to create efficiencies in operations so that a higher percentage of their funds reach the intended target of research.

Efficiency of funds spent on R&D could be increased through a global research consortium that monitors all such activity to help coordinate and guide all R&D efforts. Such a system could eliminate wasteful duplication of effort, and provide a mechanism for sharing of available research knowledge with and between the different R&D undertakings. The consortium could fund a committee of experts to track promising technologies and provide guidance in spending allocations. In sum, all viable means and methods to increase the finding of new knowledge should be utilized. The wise use of what we have now, can lead to a lean, mean, knowledge finding machine.

Chapter V
Fix the System
"Real Change"

Those who have money can make campaign donations to influence laws for their benefit. This is legal bribery, which constitutes a system design flaw. Politicians spend allot of time raising campaign funds in order to get elected or reelected, and subsequently they make promises in exchange for donations. We then have government representatives stuck in a system where they must spend time raising money by making promises and selling influence to the money givers, instead of spending time making a better world for the people. This flaw has resulted in tax credits and deductions for specific groups totaling $535 billion a year. The non-profit organization Americans For Fair Taxation, at http://www.fairtax.org or 1-800-FAIRTAX, has developed a consumption based tax plan (fair tax) for America that will eliminate all tax loopholes. This fair tax plan will raise the same amount of taxes as the current federal income tax method, but in a simpler, more equitable way that will stimulate economic growth by encouraging investment and savings, while eliminating most compliance costs of the tax system. The current estimated yearly cost to society for tracking, calculating, documenting and filing taxes is $225 billion. The fair tax system could reduce these compliance costs by as much as 95%. These potential savings in wasted resources (over $200 billion), could be reinvested in research for a better way of life. Multiply these savings by the global potential, and add savings from other wasted resource realignments, and a concerted effort toward reaching Utopia could be funded without any real sacrifice.

While there is no researched estimate of the additional costs of this legal bribery through wasted taxpayer spending on moneyed special interests (such as farm price supports), costs in terms of damages because of necessary laws not passed (such as pollution bans), and costs to consumers because of unnecessary laws passed to protect special interest groups (such as tariffs), it would be fair to estimate such costs as immense. The simple solution is to eliminate all the problems of a representative democratic system, by converting to a true democratic system. All Americans have to do is pass a constitutional amendment to reflect the changing technological capabilities available for fulfilling the self-government principles America was founded upon. We can cut out the middleman, the politicians, and use available communication mechanisms to allow each citizen of legal age to vote on which laws to pass. A true democratic evolution, provided for by the information revolution. We no longer have to rely on others to vote in our best interests, but instead can vote for ourselves. This principle should be carried up to the global level, and down to the local level. Such involvement and direct control over our destiny should revitalize each person's sense of value and self-worth.

The outline of such a system is simple. Keep the three branches of government system. The judicial system could stay the same except that the highest court in each state and the supreme court would be replaced by a system providing for decisions by majority vote. An elected committee could decide which cases to accept on appeal, public debate could ensue along with drafts of opposing opinions, and the people then vote as to how they believe the law should apply. The executive branch could be remodeled to fit the corporate method. The voters would act like shareholders and elect a board of directors, who then pick the management team (president, department heads, etc.). After each annual report on the state of affairs from an independent audit team, board members would be elected by the public from the available candidates. Congress would continue to function as oversight of the legislative branch, but their law making authority would be limited to expert proposers of laws only. Any laws proposed by congress, or from a public proposal system, would be voted on by the people, after the proposals are publicly debated as to their cost, benefit, etc. All the wasted taxpayer spending on moneyed interests, and costs of laws passed or not passed to protect these moneyed interests, can be reinvested in knowledge acquisition to further improve the Human condition. Americans have a constitutional guaranty to a government of the people, by the people, and for the people. We deserve this government of true democracy, and not the current system of government for the people who donate money to the politicians. In sum, vote for yourself, instead of voting for a politician who votes for campaign donors.

Chapter VI
Wise Spending
"Efficiency"

Government functions in a monopoly environment with no competition to weed out waste. In fact, government accounting methods encourage waste through year-end frivolous spending of excess budget funds by government departments. Runaway government spending is also fueled by unnecessary duplication of agencies. For example, six military branches, Army, Air Force, Marines, Navy, Coast Guard, National Reserve, means six administrative staffs, six payroll systems, etc. Consolidate, and instant savings. Government also wastes resources through under-utilization. For example, military personnel could assist police departments, during times of peace, by patrolling public places with the authority to make arrests should they observe a crime. In sum, there is a massive amount of waste in the way government spends tax dollars to provide services to the public.

Government should utilize methods of operation that provide the greatest efficiency in the least costly way. Government can easily learn how to utilize operational efficiencies from the business world's accumulated wisdom. One simple solution to inefficient government operations is to hire a consulting firm to study government operations and make recommendations of how to increase efficiencies and cut waste. These consulting recommendations may include necessary controls to stop fraud against government, efficient centralization of information systems for easy coordination within and between agencies, consolidation to create efficiencies and eliminate redundant costs, etc. In fact, universities and nonprofit organizations could also use consultants to increase efficiencies so that more of their funds reach the intended target.

Any savings in government spending could be used to find ways to stamp out crime, disease, pollution, etc., in order to make a better world now, without any additional sacrifice. Total annual state and federal government spending in the U.S. is $2,350,000,000,000 (2,350 billion dollars). Each 1% savings of this spending (23.5 billion dollars) could constitute a large increase in R&D funding for knowledge acquisition.

Chapter VII
Simplicity
"Common Sense"

Plain old common sense should be used in making public decisions. There is an old adage, "give a man a fish and you feed him for a day, teach a man to fish and you feed him for life." Most governmental and charitable efforts at problem solving take the "give a fish" approach. Public problem solving efforts need to be refocused toward correcting the problem causing the undesirable circumstance, instead of treating the resulting symptoms. For example, the expanding of the focus for helping the disadvantaged to gaining self-sufficiency costs a little more in the short run, but pays off in the long term. Each displaced person who achieves self-sufficiency, results in multiple positive impacts on society, because there is a happy person no longer using public funds, while producing through earning a living, and contributing to the tax base.

Additionally, more effort should be devoted to avoid public problems. Public policy is unnecessarily focused on management by putting out fires, instead of making things fire proof. It is less costly in both Human and economic terms to avoid a problem, than to fix a problem. For example, it is easier to not pollute than to clean up pollution. Public policies should take a pro-active approach, instead of a reactive approach, whenever feasible. This is a simple matter of wise planning.

In sum, let's use wisdom to avoid problems, and to solve the problems not avoided. As our knowledge increases, we will have expanded capabilities for problem resolution and/or avoidance. For example, Humanity may discover most, if not all, antisocial harmful behavior is the result of mental disease, and may find a cure. Each such solution has a multiplier effect, in that people are no longer subjected to the negative effects of the problem solved, the quality of life is improved, and the resources that had been consumed because of the problem can be used in other ways to further improve the human condition.

Chapter VIII
Roots
"Mother Nature"

The earth is one large interconnected ecological system. People are part of this system and must currently rely on it for survival, by breathing its oxygen, drinking its water, etc. If this system can no longer provide these life-sustaining functions, Humanity will no longer exist. We should recognize our oneness with our environment, and our unity with all life on earth. The globe is the house Humanity resides in, yet we are trashing the same like drunken adolescents at a large party. This attitude of indifference is best exemplified by the fact that Humanity waged two world wars just in the last century, not to mention numerous other wars. This lack of respect of a life form for itself, would explain its lack of respect for other life forms, which includes the living earth. As a human, I must admit I am totally ashamed of this aspect of our species. On an individual level, most people are very nice and caring. Collectively, we should be the same. Every individual can develop a respect for their life, learn how to appreciate the beauty and sanctity of all life, and recognize the oneness of being part of the same. We should then be able to find this individual good in our collective actions.

There are many current ways knowledge can help Humanity

live as one with the world, such as energy conservation, recycling, etc. We need better coordination of such efforts, and dissemination of this knowledge for use now. Part of the solution is to decrease Humanity's demand on the environment. An increase in global population of 78,000,000 (78 million) per year indicates it is time to work on population control. Education, economic disincentive, better birth control methods, and/or other ways should be used to reduce growth in population and alleviate the increasing strain on nature's systems. Trees absorb carbon dioxide and produce oxygen, which is a reduction of gasses from the burning of fossil fuels and an increase in clean air. Therefore, a simple partial solution is a global tree planting campaign. We can use better development methods that preserve more land in its natural state, etc. Since we do not yet have the benefit of future knowledge, we must simply do the best we can at peaceful interfacing with nature now, while seeking better methods for the future.

Let's wise up and obtain the new knowledge to fulfill our needs while preserving the beauty and sanctity of nature. We must find the ability to live as one with the world. For example, agricultural pollution is the most prolific form of pollution, yet knowledge will provide the solution to this pollution, through genetic engineering of plants that may alleviate the need for pesticides, and/or natural means to use as countermeasures to disrupt breeding of insects, and/or through some other method or methods. Manufacturing pollution may be eliminated through means to recycle this pollution in some useful non-harmful manner, or by enzymes and bacteria that break toxins and pollutants back down into basic non-harmful elements. In sum, with increased individual awareness, proficient use of current knowledge, and further research, the world will learn to live as one.

Chapter IX
Try
"Sing the Song of Change"

The simple reality is that all systems made by humans, can be changed by humans. Every person has some influence upon the people with whom they have regular contact, and those people have influence with others, and the others have influence on people they know, who in turn have influence etc., which means each individual can influence the world through their actions. The total of all Human actions determines whether the world is like a heaven on earth, or a living hell. Everyone makes a vote as to the type of world we have with their lifetime efforts. One can influence these voting results by stuffing the ballot box with an increase in the number and size of actions for change. The most important decision one makes with their life, is the course of action they will take with their life.

The very least an individual can do for a better world is to be a good and productive citizen. This simply involves focusing on the positive part within oneself, and avoiding the negative side. Like a movie where you root for the good guy over the bad guy, just root for yourself to be a good guy in real life.

The next level of involvement is to join in the dialogue for a better world. This is a simple matter of communication.

The highest level of involvement is to spend some time and/or money toward making a positive difference. There are many simple actions that people can engage in at this level with little sacrifice, but great reward. The type and amount of one's involvement for a better world is purely a personal choice. Donate some time and/or money to one or more of the many noble organizations devoted to making the world a better place. Get involved with one of these organizations, or start a new one. Write a representative about a better world, or run for political office on a better world platform. Get involved with your community, or start your own Utopian community. Increase your knowledge and/or facilitate the education of others. Discover wasteful spending that can be redirected toward R&D. Donate to research, or become a researcher. There are many ways to contribute. Simply choose your way, or ways, and do it.

One caveat is that the Utopian evolution is a peaceful transformation, and any actions toward the same must only be positive actions. Therefore, negative actions with the intent to get positive results are inappropriate, unnecessary, and a violation of the Utopian principle.

Like a chorus, the more people who sing the song, the louder the sound waves resonate. Join the chorus for change. Everyone has the chance to leave an everlasting imprint on mankind. Make the most of this opportunity by being the best you can be in your interactions throughout life. A noble direction in life rewards the individual with a feeling of satisfaction and fulfillment from the act of giving a pure and true gift, while resulting in a better world to increase the enjoyment of the noble life.

Chapter X
Summation
"Nurture the Seed"

At this point in time, Utopia is just the seed of an idea.

With the right nurturing, that seed will grow into something beautiful.

A simple message of hope, that can be fulfilled by a unified effort.

THE ULTIMATE PHILOSOPHY - BOOK III

Visions

Introduction

The first book, The Ultimate Philosophy - Book I, set forth a practical theory of how to merge Utopia with reality.

The second book, The Ultimate Philosophy - Book II, set forth some actual methods for merging Utopia with reality.

This third book completes a philosophical trilogy on Utopia by exploring some perceptions of Utopia.

Table of Contents

Chapter I   Being
Chapter II   Paradox
Chapter III   Already There
Chapter IV   Neighbors
Chapter V   Spirituality
Chapter VI   Futurists
Chapter VII Evolution
Chapter VIII Perfect Picture
Chapter IX   Energy
Chapter X   Summation

Chapter I
Being
"Human Duality"

Visions of Utopia are as numerous as the number of people. Every person has their own view of what Utopia, a heaven on earth, would be like. While there is no unified view of Utopia, the various views can be classified into some common groups. The range of these groups spans from those who believe they have already found Utopia, to those who believe humans can reach a state of pure energy, which is a realm beyond Utopia.

All views of Utopia involve change, which affects human systems and institutions. Such change will only be facilitated by a fundamental reassessment of every human-made system in light of its purpose and function. For example, enforcement of the law should refocus its goal to truth finding, and eliminate the institutionalized court room rules that perpetuate gamesmanship instead of justice. Some people are blinded by emotion and/or self-serving beliefs when it comes to changing institutions or systems they are connected with. Institutions exist to serve humans. Humans do not exist to serve institutions. The starting point of an honest evaluation of the systems that serve Humanity is an understanding of who they serve, which involves an understanding of the nature of humans.

Humans consist of a physical body which includes the brain. The cells of the body and brain are interconnected by nerve fibers. These nerve fibers carry nerve impulses from the brain to the body, and stimulus from the sensory organs (eyes, ears, nose, tongue, and skin) to the brain. The body is nourished with food, and burns the same to create the energy impulses that travel the nerves. Therefore, people are part of the duality of the third dimension.

Three-dimensional objects (matter) are in essence trapped energy, and as such, mass can be converted into energy, and energy can be converted into mass. Einstein's theory of relativity summarizes this duality by stating that matter and energy are not distinct, and they can be changed into each other (energy is equivalent to mass times the velocity of light squared). One example of this duality is photosynthesis. The sun emits energy in the form of light and heat by burning up matter, and trees convert the sun light back into matter in the form of their growth. A grown tree may then be burned in a fireplace to release energy in the form of heat and light. This circular duality between energy and matter is one of the elements of the third dimension. The human mind is at the cusp of this duality. The brain functions at the convergence between matter and energy, and uses energy to create thought. The human body (mass) is the tangible physical existence, and thought (energy impulses traveling in that mass) is the intangible mental existence. The duality of mass and energy exist in man as body and thought.

The body is a vessel only. Once the brain stops functioning, there is a lack of energy impulses, one is legally dead, and if on life support machines they are disconnected because the body alone is not the person. One's being is their conscious perception of themselves and their surroundings, which perception comprises current sensory impulses in conjunction with accessed knowledge from prior stored memories in the brain. In sum, the true essence of being is mental existence through thought from energy.

Chapter II
Paradox
"Sensory Filters"

The Human thought process is not a perfect mechanism. Human sensory organs act as filters of knowledge, because they can only pass along information that they have the ability to detect. That sensory information is further restricted by the limits of the body's information delivery systems, and the limits of the brain's faculty for perception of information so delivered. Thought is affected by feelings and emotions such as, love-hate, excited-bored, happy-sad, funny-serious, euphoric-depressed, etc. Thought can be affected by mental illness. People have varying levels of intelligence, and intelligence can manifest itself selectively as with idiot savants. Chemicals released by the body, or ingested, can affect thought processes. As a result of evolutionary survival mechanisms, personality traits and characteristics are influenced by one's genetic composition (DNA). In sum, thought processes are complex mechanisms. Humanity currently lacks complete knowledge of exactly how the thought process works, and therefore lacks complete control over the same.

Without a complete understanding of thought processes, and methods to completely control the same, Humanity can never have a true Utopia. Under current circumstances people can be placed in a perfect environment, but there will still be hatred, jealousy, and other manifestations of negative thoughts and actions. In short, a perfect environment will not provide a perfect existence for an imperfect being. It is a paradox for an imperfect being to seek a perfect existence by seeking a perfect place. Therefore, Utopia is more than a place, it is a state of being that fulfills both sides of human duality.

In order to reach Utopia we must be able to perfect not just our environment, but also ourselves. Like control of the environment through technology, our ability to control thought processes is a necessary piece of the Utopian puzzle. We need a "pair of docs" (two doctors), one to fix our environment, and one to fix ourselves. Once we can control and regulate negative thoughts, and obtain the ability to have pure thought unrestrained by limitations, we will be free from the chains of our imperfect state of being, and able to reach higher levels of being. We will see the light instead of shadows.

In light of this basic understanding of what a human-being is, some common perceptions of Utopia are assessed in the following chapters.

Chapter III
Already There
"Peace and Love"

Some people believe Humanity can have Utopia now. They believe Humanity has everything necessary for a Utopia, and that humans just have to better utilize what they have now and enjoy the same. The World Game Institute has prepared the most comprehensive statement of this position and posted the same at http://www.worldgame.org/wwwproject/index.shtml The Institute has identified various programs and policies that could provide for food, water, shelter, health care, energy and education for every person in the world, while eliminating all major environmental problems. Without a solution, more than 800 million people will remain malnourished, large segments of the population will continue to suffer from preventable diseases, and over 40 million people will die each year from starvation or preventable diseases. Additionally, plant and animal extinction, deforestation, soil erosion, ozone depletion, and other major environmental problems will continue. The combined total cost of implementing corrective programs is 30% of the world's total annual military expenditures, or 234 billion dollars. Society's by-standing at this mass human slaughter because of improper use of available resources constitutes complicity in murder. If one is not convinced of the imperative need to solve such problems for humanitarian reasons, then it should be noted that the resulting benefits of an overall enhanced quality of life, increased global productivity, and environmental preservation, clearly exceed the costs of these programs.

Being in tune with ourselves and nature, and wisely using our current resources is an excellent start for having a better world. Life is full of wonder and beauty and should be cherished and enjoyed by everyone. However, Humanity can, and should, do better, such as finding cures for all disease.

Chapter IV
Neighbors
"Utopian Communities"

Some Utopia seekers think Humanity's problems can be solved by community level autonomy and self-rule. They believe each community should be free to set its own standards and rules and that there should be a community for each different type of belief and preference that exists. Each community would establish its own rules of conduct and behavior, allowing any conduct and behavior preferred, and prohibiting any conduct and behavior disliked. Subsequently, each person can pick a community to live in which matches their vision of an ideal community. For instance, one community may be vegetarian only with legalized drugs; another may be a community of open sexual relations with no family structure recognized; or a community may be of families only with a particular religious belief; etc. Each person could live the style of life they personally choose, and could do so in an environment where other lifestyles that they believe are offensive are not allowed. Like exclusive social clubs, there could be exclusive communities of people with common behavioral standards. If one desires variety of beliefs then there would be a community to accommodate such like-minded people. Whatever ones desires, preferences, and beliefs, there would be a community for such like-minded people. Of course for those who want to live alone, so be it.

Other people believe a Utopia civilization can be achieved by having a community that is properly structured and operated. Numerous attempts, both past and present, have been undertaken to build Utopian communities. These are noble, well-intentioned efforts, that may bring a happier than otherwise attainable life to their residents, but none have achieved their goal, because Utopia is more than a place, it is a state of being. These communities seek the solution to all human problems through a perfect living environment, which is just one side of the Utopian equation. The solution to human imperfection must also be found in order to have Utopia.

Chapter V
Spirituality
"Supernatural"

Some claim that an unseen force or level of existence will provide instant nirvana and/or solve all human problems. There are a multitude of different types of such claims. All one has to do to have the alleged benefit of any such claim is join a group, accept certain beliefs, buy informational tapes or books, and/or pay to attend seminars. In exchange for personal and financial commitments, one will allegedly be shown how to live at some higher level and/or use the power of that higher plane of existence. The only higher power at work here is the manipulation of people for the green god better known as money. None of these claims are scientifically verifiable, and as such they are a bunch of mumbo jumbo. There is no unseen magic that will solve all human problems.

The only true spirit humans have access to is the human spirit, which is the power from human attributes and qualities. That power is no mystery, but simply the ability to conceptualize something, and the desire and will to make the same a reality. Humanity must use this spirit to learn all that it can about itself and its environment, in order to discover how to control and regulate the same for the highest quality of life possible.

Humanity is continually enhancing its abilities, such as the power of creation through cloning, genetic engineering, test tube babies, etc. The ability to create is just one of the godlike abilities Humanity is obtaining, and through such abilities Humanity is evolving toward a godlike existence. In the beginning there was man, and created he the concept of god. Humans are becoming what they dreamed of.

Chapter VI
Futurists
"Environmental Mastery"

The most common Utopian belief is that Humanity will reach Utopia by acquiring powerful technological abilities, while human physiology and characteristics remain essentially the same. Nanotechnology is the most revolutionary of currently conceived future technological abilities. Nanotechnology is simply molecular manufacturing. A nanometer is one billionth of a meter, so nanomachines would exist at an infinitesimal scale. All matter (gases, liquids, and solid objects) is composed of molecules, and molecules are just specific combinations of atoms. Atoms are composed of electrons, protons, and neutrons. Molecular assemblers, microscopic machines, would build molecules by putting atoms together. Just give this machine any type of matter, such as water, and it can rearrange the atomic pieces to make anything else, such as an apple, or gold. These nanomachines can even make copies of themselves, so that once one is built, Humanity can have all the nanomachines it wants. Every home could have a machine, consisting of a very large quantity of these microscopic nanomachines, to provide for all material needs. For example, if you want a glass of orange juice simply tell the machine and it can use water from a water line connection to make a glass filled with orange juice. When you are finished drinking the juice, just put the glass in the machine, and the machine will turn the glass back into clean water and send the water down the drain. People will never have to shop again. New clothes, caviar, lobster, no problem, just tell the machine to make whatever is wanted. These nanomachines will build miniature super-computers, and robots of any desired size. People will not have to work because these robots, computers and machines, will be able to perform any task that needs to be done, or is desired to be done. However, if one desires to work, these production methods can be used to create any work environment one desires. Material poverty will be eliminated. Money, a medium of exchange for material goods and services, will become obsolete, because every individual can have all of their material needs and desires fulfilled by this unlimited production capability. Taxes are no longer necessary. Nanomachines can patrol the human body killing viruses, deleting any cancerous growths, and regenerating damaged cells so that one never ages or gets sick. Pollution will not result from this molecular manufacturing process, and these nanomachines can be unleashed to clean up any preexisting pollution. There is no need to harvest trees, or other natural resources, because nanomachines can make anything desired. Animals will not have to be raised for slaughter to feed humans or provide clothes, because nanomachines can make anything desired. This unlimited production system just needs matter and energy to function. These machines can make solar panels and energy storage devices so efficient that the energy from the sun will be the only power ever needed. The only other thing needed to run the machines is some type of matter, which can be air, water, dirt, or anything else that is plentiful. Fantastic engineering feats are possible, such as see-through domes over cities to eliminate weather concerns, and an extensive water piping system to eliminate drought and floods. Extraordinary amusement parks and entertainment centers could be built with this technology. Space exploration and colonization would be easily feasible with this technology. Whole planets can be encased in a protective see-through shield and a vacation paradise or living space can be created on them.

In sum, through some combination of machines, robots, computers, and/or other technologies, Humanity will have the ability to provide for all material needs and desires, and Humanity can thereby make and/or create any environment desired. Humanity will be able to build perfect places.

Chapter VII
Evolution
"Mental Mastery"

Humanity will develop methods to control and regulate feelings and emotions, increase intelligence, and eliminate mental illness. People will have a mental heaven through mind-shaping. People will have healthy minds free from any mental agony such as depression, because all mental illness will be cured. Humans will discover how to access and unleash the full capabilities and power of the brain, and thereby reach levels of intelligence and thought that takes the essence of being to an unimaginably complete state of existence. Humanity will be able to achieve control of the brain so one can elect to have any feeling or emotion desired, or elect to avoid any feeling or emotion. One will be able to have pure thought unaffected by feelings or emotions, and unrestrained by sensory or other limitations. Such mind-shaping methods may involve the use of chemicals and/or genetic engineering to enhance the pleasure pathways of the brain, and block negative feedback pathways. This would result is a perpetual state of happiness, pleasure, and joy. Boredom, anger and other negative feelings and emotions will no longer plague humans. People will be happy about being in a state of happiness, a perpetual love of everything. Each individual will have the capability to completely control their thoughts, and thereby be the god of their own universe, the king of their mental sphere of existence.

Additionally, Humanity will develop sensory devices to enhance mental abilities, and virtual reality systems for unlimited mental experiences. The virtual reality systems will allow people to experience anything desired, and it will be and feel as if it actually happened. For example, instead of reading a novel, one can live the story in a three-dimensional perception that cannot be distinguished from reality. Through virtual systems one can experience anything they can conceptualize. Everyone would have their own unlimited mental amusement park, and the experiences can be interactive with other humans. Total freedom exists in such a world where one's virtual actions cannot cause harm or damage to anything real. For example, one could go on a mental safari and have the experience of bagging big game, yet cause no harm. There are no limits or rules in virtual land. In such a place, even the sky is not the limit because one can fly like an eagle if they so desire. The sensory devices will allow people to experience a plethora of new perceptions, and reach levels of ecstasy and other feelings beyond current human ability. Such sensory devices can heighten and enhance any feeling or perception. Some of the new feelings achieved may even make the orgasmic feeling seem dull by comparison. In fact the enhanced and expanded sensational experiences may be so blissful that people will give up the hassle of maintaining a body as a vessel, and have their brain downloaded into a computer or have their brain placed in some form of a virtual sensory nutrient tank for perpetual existence at the heightened level of perception. There is some empirical evidence of such a desirability from studies which show lab rats will forgo even food in order to sustain electric stimulation of the pleasure area of their brain.

A key caveat of mind-shaping is that society should not be able to require or restrict any such capabilities, and that the individual should have complete personal choice and control over what, if any, mind-shaping they will undergo.

In sum, through some method or combination of methods, Humanity will have the ability to provide for all mental needs and desires. Humans will be able to achieve full mental satisfaction through utilization of maximum intellectual capabilities, the curing of all mental illness, elimination of the negative side of human nature, and virtual sensory devices. Such full mental satisfaction will have profound positive impacts on current paradigms. For example, drug abuse, crime, and war may become obsolete because mentally satisfied people have no need or desire to engage in such activities; and/or this higher level of increased conscious-being may usher in an era of peaceful coexistence where the need for social rules dissipates; and/or etc. However, the full scope of any such impacts is beyond the limit of Humanity's current level of knowledge.

Chapter VIII
Perfect Picture
"?"

Our ability to control our environment and ourselves will increase and through some combination of such abilities each individual will be able to live in their vision of heaven. This picture of Utopia is the ability of each person to live in their own picture of Utopia. A heaven on earth, where everyone lives as they desire. In order to satisfy all people Utopia cannot be a "one size fits all" environment, but must be a multitude of different environments concept. A true Utopia must be everything to everyone, and, as such, must contain the five basic elements set forth in the first book of this trilogy. As to the element of complete knowledge, Humanity will eventually obtain a complete understanding of how it and everything in its proximate environment works, and learn methods to control and regulate the same. Once the complete knowledge element is obtained, any other element can be satisfied. As to the element of everlasting life, Humanity will eventually learn how to eliminate death and illness. As to the element of all good and no evil, evil will be eliminated because Humanity will learn how to discard its negative side. As to the infinite provision element, Humanity will develop unlimited production capabilities to provide for all material needs and desires, and methods will be discovered to satisfy all mental needs and desires.

Excluding the as of yet unknown impact of future full mental satisfaction capabilities on the individual-society paradigm, the fifth element, a perfect balance between the individual and society, is the most problematic. Utopia is a true freedom concept. True freedom includes not only the right of free choice, but also the ability to exercise the right of free choice. True freedom permeates all aspects of life, and is more comprehensive than any current philosophy of freedom. Such freedom must include environmental mastery that will allow one freedom from having to work to provide for material needs, freedom from illness and disease, and freedom from death which is the ultimate restriction on life. Such freedom must include mental mastery that will free people from anguish, sadness and other negative mental experiences, and allow people to break the chains of sensory and intellectual limitations. However, when interacting with other humans the freedom to do as you please also includes the right of others not to be offended by your actions and vice versa. One way to satisfy all parties when balancing the right of individual freedom against the right of people not to be annoyed, injured, or offended by actions of others, is to allow any activity, but restrict where the activity may be engaged in. Clearly one should have total freedom inside their own home. When one wants to interact with other humans, in a real setting, they should be able to select the environment that has the rules they prefer. Instead of standard rules for all public places, society could establish different rules for different places so that each person can go to the type of public place where there are rules of conduct and behavior that suits their preference. There could be a varying mixture of rules of conduct for different public places which results in at least one easily accessible place to satisfy any particular type of mixture of desired public behavior. For example, nudists who like to swill beer, smoke stogies, curse, and listen to loud rock bands, should have a public place to go to that suits their desires, and people who are offended by such behavior would know to avoid that place. Under such a system there is total freedom, except for the harm to life prohibition, and except for some restrictions on where some conduct may be engaged in. Actually, even a harm to life desire can be fulfilled, either through virtual reality, or with lifelike robotic forms. All needs and desires can be fulfilled, there are just some restrictions on where it may be done.

Chapter IX
Energy
"Beyond Utopia"

Humanity may discover a way to exist as pure energy, a form of pure thought. It is in this place beyond Utopia, Entopia, where the need for any restrictions becomes obsolete. This theoretical highest level of existence is beyond the scope of anything humans can currently experience. Such a state of being should allow for unlimited mental ability, where one would experience omnipotence. In such a state of existence, there are no boundaries of essence, and no restrictions on being. In such a pure state of being there are no problems, worries, or negative concerns. Such a state of being would be a type of ultimate content peaceful completeness. If Humanity can reach such a state, it will have checkmated nature.

Chapter X
Summation
"Seek and Ye Shall Find"

The future is an unknown quantity, and as such can only be speculated about. Utopia could be some form of one of the above methods, some other method beyond Humanity's current ability of perception, or some combination thereof. What is known, is that the present state of the world is not the best Humanity can do, and neither was the past. We must press forward to find our best. There are no limits to future abilities, just limits to what we can do now. We simply must keep shining the light of knowledge on the darkness of ignorance, until we find our best. If we continue on such a path, at some point in the future, Humanity will bridge the gap between reality and Utopia.

Thank you for your time, and may your life be Utopian.

CONCLUSION

Since everyone desires a good life,
we should make the same a common goal,
and devote some more resources toward finding the
knowledge to make it a reality for all.

A simple plan to make a dream come true.

EPILOGUE

To be determined by the Human Race

*The Real Utopian Earthborn
Believes In Better Life Everlasting*

Printed in the United States
773400002B